when water turns to vapor

Advance Praise

"In when water turns to vapor, Joy Bickham poignantly shares her journey of life, infertility, loss, pregnancy after loss, and motherhood through a collection of poetry. Written as she walks through these events in her life, the collection is raw and authentic. The recurring themes of faith, pain, and hope carry through the book, letting readers know they are not alone as they walk their own paths through loss and life after. This moving collection of poetry and Joy Bickham's story validates the pain from pregnancy loss and is a soothing companion for those experiencing their own loss journeys."
—Valerie R. Meek
Operations Director of *Pregnancy After Loss Support*

"In this collection, Joy takes the brutal subjects of infertility and miscarriage, effortlessly interweaving them with grace and faith, fearlessly sharing her own journey towards motherhood so that others will know they are not alone. Beautiful."
—Lynn Renee Maxcy
Screenwriter, *The Handmaid's Tale* on Hulu

"Rich in the details of lived sensory experience and the metaphors of revealed truth, when water turns to vapor weaves together grief, faith, and intense reflection to create the personal mythology of a woman's body in the midst of miscarriage, infertility, and motherhood."
—Marcus Chinn
Father and Husband, *Voice from the Void* Poet

"Having been in ministry for over twenty years, I have had numerous opportunities to see heartache and disappointment in the lives of those I've ministered to and in my own life. Unfortunately, the Church, as a whole, has not done a good job at giving people room to ask questions or grieve losses. In doing so, we rob people from the opportunity to discover the faithfulness of Jesus in the midst of that pain. In this collection of poetic thoughts, Joy has put words to the tears I have experienced and invited others to the intimate details of her own questions. The raw emotion and honest questions she penned, open a door for others who also have walked this road. This open door will give people a chance to experience a depth of God they would never have known. I pray this will give others the hope they need to move forward and the courage to share their own stories. "

—Pastor Jodi Rodgers
Director of Student Ministries, *New Season Christian Fellowship*

when water turns to vapor

a poetry journey of love, loss, and life

Joy R. Bickham

when water turns to vapor
a poetry journey of love, loss, and life

To request permissions, contact the publisher at punandquill.wordpress.com

Cover design by Joy R. Bickham

ISBN: 9798822203259

This book is dedicated to Bryce, who has faithfully followed through with three words that I desperately needed to hear:

"I'm with you."

Foreword
By Bekah Thompson

Having babies is not everyone's calling. This is a truth I've come to know. However, that's not everyone's truth. And that's a bit of the point of this book, to share someone's truth which might be different from yours.

As a parent, I tell people that *I never knew fear until I had a child*. For my sister Joy, the same could be said for the process of having a child.

Joy was one of my first siblings married, one of the first to endure the pressures and expectation of growing a family. We grew up together in a household of seven siblings, one by one leaving the nest and married successfully per our mother's greatest prayer. Joy's fertility journey could not be more of a juxtaposition from my own. She and her husband were married for quite a few years before they decided they wanted to grow their family. When I was married, my husband and I started our family within a year and I was pregnant within a week of attempting to conceive. At that time, I wasn't even sure I was ready but found myself pregnant almost immediately. While Joy has endured the challenges and pain of just trying to get pregnant, I had already gone through pregnancy and experienced the pleasures and challenges of parenting.

Although I may never really experience the type of loss and grief Joy and Bryce have endured, I did witness glimpses: the cautious excitement of pregnancy, the vulnerability of their hope, the anxiety of waiting, the anguish of their loss and the weariness of the cycle repeated. It humbled me and I felt guilty with the truth that honestly, I don't know that I could carry the level of perseverance required to walk the road they did had I been faced with the same obstacles in my path towards having a baby. In that regard, I have a deep respect and empathy for her and what she and her husband endured over the years.

The path to having a child is one that can be very individual, intimate, and challenging for some, or open, easy, and exciting for others. Having worked closely with single moms and their children who were experiencing homelessness, I've had the unique experience of observing firsthand the burden of responsibility that can be unfairly thrust upon the them. I understand this is not everyone's story and it is sobering to be in a place to have a choice, to be earnestly wanting something and working for it and prepared for the responsibility of it. Yet at the same time, it can be full of pain and obstacles in a different way.

For the longest time, I had not fully realized the extent and scope of Joy's loss until the day she shared with me the inked image she chose to imprint on her body. The tattoo beautifully adorns her skin, displayed in a visible area on her forearm. Like the pages of this book, the image invites a willing observer to hear her story and the meaning of the symbolism her body now bears - one of hope, vulnerability, joy, and loss.

Writing has always been an incredible source of power for Joy, a solace of her creative energies. In this book she reveals her darkest moments and brings visibility to the pain of infertility of those who might be carrying the burden of a similar story.

Joy will remind you of the bravery, strength and diligence required in the fertility process and that not every road to children is a joyful one. Using a pregnancy test can be an action of hope or angst for two very different outcomes, and both journeys can be painful but important to understand. There is a strength in sharing our vulnerability and truth with others. And like the badge of Joy's tattoo, I see this collection of poems as a symbol of Joy's truth and strength.

May the words read throughout this book encourage compassion and empathy to readers who may not have experienced loss. May it provide comfort to those who see themselves in the pages of these poems. And may you, like Joy, find strength in the support and love of those you surround yourselves with should you ever have to face personal tragedy.

Table of Contents

Preface

In the summer of 2018, I lost my first baby during pregnancy week 10. Its birth date would have been January 18, 2019.

Valentine's Day 2019, I found out I was pregnant with my second baby. I experienced another loss at week 5 of pregnancy.

After my two losses, I underwent a number of fertility tests and was diagnosed with Polycystic Ovarian Syndrome (PCOS) and Hypothyroidism.

On July 4th, 2020, during the first year of the COVID-19 Pandemic, I found out I was pregnant with my third baby.

Despite levels–upon–levels of fear, but with amazing support from fellow survivors in my Pregnancy After Loss Support group, I emerged in 2021 with a healthy baby boy who I thank God is celebrating his 19th month as of this writing.

https://pregnancyafterlosssupport.org/get-support/pals-private-groups/

Infertility, loss, and hope. The nuances of these words will differ between each and every reader. May you find more solidarity than trauma triggers herein.

For readers who have not had these experiences, may you understand one person's perspective and may it grow your compassion for the many. Approximately 1 in 4 known pregnancies end in loss.

Reference: https://www.ncbi.nlm.nih.gov/books/NBK532992/

The Beginning

when water turns to vapor

Crowding

4/9/12

Dreaming drains me

Your dreams

I listen

I share

Your dreams

Hopeful, joyful, creative future

But tired face today

Waning energy

Excitement in the background

But emotions crowding up front

Up to my eyes where I feel heat and sadness

Wasn't sure what today would be

But now I can see me stepping back

Being quiet

Being secret

Like I always am
inclined

Yet there is real inspiration

And fabric patterns, textures, colors

Friendship

Work

And hopefully reward for our art and labor

But today was the first face-to-face

And my gifts and sober judgment dictates me to assist,
to support, to organize thoughts, ideas, structure

A plan

A next step

And maybe my ideas are too predictable

And maybe I have to guard my mind from summing
this all up with everything else

And naming myself and my art as unspecial

Joy is with children

Not having to be an adult

Until you feel you're ready for reality and realize you know too much and the magic is gone

Today I had a taste of something good

But it left a bad aftertaste and I am fighting fear and sadness

Jesus I trust you

Your love for me is so great and strong nothing can stop you

Let me just be

Whatever it looks like

Empty Air

4/27/13

Knees to her chest. Eyes swollen with salty drops. How can it be? After all these years, the longing is still an ocean wave. Destructive. Surrounding. The loss, a constant fresh burning. Just waiting in the background. Coming into focus again. The empty years. The stolen moments. All that's left is her talking to the empty air as if he's there. But there's another way. A letting go, as if you weren't entitled to the life you imagine.

Haiku

1/6/15

Love does not tire, no

when you nourish it daily

Hold back not a thing

Haiku 2

1/7/15

A glowing beach wave

Some bioluminescence

I wish you would stay

Time Machine

3/24/15

The smell of play dough and I'm nowhere near

My memory sense is a time machine here

Just a thought of a smell, and I'm light years away

A child again in a whole other state

Everything and Nothing

4/22/15

Saying everything, saying nothing

Saying everything, saying nothing

I was a tween in my room

The other side of the wall vibrating with hot words

When He spoke to me

Through the book of Job

That's when I read the Bible the first time through

I was a teen in the east

The other side of the world writhing in labor

When He spoke through me

Through the songs of my heart

That's when I felt His company the first time through

I was a young woman in the Sahara

The other side of my world writing with notes

When He championed me

And showed Himself Grand

That's when I learned His Depths a new way through

I was a young woman in my hometown

The other side of myself awakening in expressions

When He gifted me

And answered my prayers

That's when I learned a new facet of His love

I am a woman in my career now

The other side of life churning out its song

And He walks with me

And shows me who I am

This is how I know He is Faithful

Saying everything, saying nothing

Saying everything, saying nothing

Without a Word

5/12/15

Emotionally exhausted tied to physical exhaustion tied
to pain in shoulders, back, hips

Longing for joy

Nothing left to give

I collapse at home, too weak to do the routine

Eat, sleep, repeat

Want to dream of respite, but it's ever changing and
not my choices

Decisions made for me like an old man without a word
as his wife conducts his life

Equilibrium

10/5/15

Depression is like a weight around the neck

I drag it home and around the weekend, knocking my husband with it in the process

Depression is made up of circumstance and biology

Chemistry and events

A work pressure here

A hormone surge there

Tied in a little red bow

The stress and the timing of multiple things at once

They drag my shoulders down

Or up to my ears

Tighter and tighter until my back pops out and my head and neck cut my nerves

My mind grapples for numbness, distractions, or big changes

Throwing all efforts into running away

But around the corner you promise me there is a day
that doesn't feel like this

Soon, you say, I will return to joy and equilibrium

Until then, you're firmly by my side

Walking through this valley

With your shoulder sharing the burden

And with a banner of love announced over me

Space

11/8/15

I felt the distance between us when I went outside today.

Like the atmosphere of space

I felt weightless,

Empty.

Indoors, I feel it in my head,

But in the open courtyard

In the middle

In the green

Under the clear blue stretched above me for miles and miles and

zoomed out in a bird's-eye view

all the hours away to where you are...

It was physical.

The air surrounding me:

Tangible distance.

My fingers are numb and vacant.

The breath in my lungs is shallow,

Uneven.

Unbalanced are my biological functions

All because you aren't here.

What the Good Girl Did

12/10/15

No One wants to hear what the good girl did

No sordid stories nor tantalizing tales

No one is caught raptured in her woven yarn

Chairs empty when the lore of she is read

And maybe she would have it no other way

But the world – I tell you, dammit –

The universe needs her stories

The Defrosting

1/7/16

Warm isn't as delicious as it can be until you've spent the morning in the icy air with white puffs of condensation rising from your words and liquid drops seeping down the inner part of your nostrils. Not as delicious unless you have been bathed in the weather that turns noses red and fingers white. That prickles your cheeks and ears, and cuts through your layers of cloth. This is when the perfect warmness of coming inside and drinking hot cider replenishes your vigor as it wakes you up, sliding down your throat, heating as it goes.

Letting Go

1/29/16

Young Christian men talking about helping children, attending church gives a sense of relief from some things I didn't know I was carrying—a deep conviction that the world was lost. Overhearing their joy in simple life plans splashes light on my face.

Perfect perch: in the cool corner red couch with just enough sunlight on the coffee mug pressed to my chest to keep me warm, light that isn't directly on my page lest it be washed out, a sound track of good years in my ears, lyrics like buttered brandy to my soul. Choice phrases reflect emotions I believed about myself.

I'm in a grand mood.

Then the ballpoint pen presses a blue divot in the journal page and composes…

"A little head bounced into view as a new father passed by the window where she worked. She punched her earbuds deep into her ears and swiped to a ragey song.

She started her f-ing, damn period today and didn't know she wanted to be a mom until that very instant.

There are not too many days that a monumental life realization comes to wash over us like a strong breeze running into, through, and around us.

And, it's hard not to take it personally when an evil spirit walks up to you and spits in your face.

Both are things you can't control, and there is something supreme in letting go."

Pinching

2/1/16

Disappointment—is that the right word? Maybe "woundedness"—pinches my sides together and aches my heart, reminiscent of a toddler who didn't get her way. A feeling of being picked up under the arms like a two year old, moved away and scolded. Feels like someone decided to pull me back from my goal, as if I don't have control over reaching my dreams. "But I'm a bloody adult!" I shouldn't need to feel this residue of discipline. This stain in my emotional memory—connecting childhood to adulthood—and painting me as juvenile, marking me as belt-whipped in my own mind.

I'm embarrassed and angry, hurt, and blind to the careless attitude I was in hours before I read your email, "Don't patronize me. Only tell me the truth."

Burning

2/16/16

My non-stick pan is getting sticky.

Food glued to the middle.

Half my dinner is burning,

but still I stir,

stir.

Settle

5/12/16

Settle settle

Pressure down upon my jitters

Until I am still

A fragrant pie cooling on a window sill

Heat escaping in tiny swirls

And the juices solidify and flavors meld

The fruit, it settles settles settles

Too often I am on a bike

Ever pushing, pressing in forward motion

Grab my bars to a halt

Calm my beating heart

Hold down my pedals

Help me settle settle

I want to be chill

An icebox treat for a summer thrill

A cooling pie on a window sill

A carefree day would fit the bill

Settle

Settle

Settle

SIX

7/11/16

1

A rush of salt water and goose pimples

I pad my feathers rapidly to reach air

dripping, blurry

stuffed, ringing

I cough

Unprepared, although I've intentionally built my latest dwelling on the beach

For on the crest of danger is where the sunrise gleams

I might've been better off to piecemeal a nest in the awning uphill

Where only the sticky wet breeze can sway me

But I may lull there too long and forget to awaken to day

Lost in the subtleties of shady monotone

2

Hangars clink together

The rhythmic cycle of wash, dry, hang

has got me in a trance

Reach, pull, bend, throw,

bend, grab, reach

The warmth from the dryer

The damp from the washer

And the many–type fabrics running 'cross the tips of my fingers

I hardly noticed you standing there

Until your arms gently slide around me

And you hold your sweetness next to me in a soft embrace

A silent 'thank you'

3

Soon we'll be in 80 degrees

Scanning the skyline of mountains and fields

Hearing nothing but wind rustling the rough spiky grasses

Acres away, acres away

Familiar loved faces

Jokes and discoveries

Food and games

And reflections of pride

Loving our Father

And thankful for country

As fireworks burst

on the Fourth of July

4

It's done

I'm done

Finished with a project

The relief of out of my hands

Of waiting for feedback

Done

It's done

No more hours hunched over crafting the page,
selecting perfect language and form

I'm left with a sense of accomplishment, of pride

5

Pails of pride

Pile high the sands of memories into a castle on the shore

A flag of red, blue, and white

Strikes my gut instinct to throw up a prayer of grateful thanks

Huddling together under the stars and beside the firelight of roasting sweets

6

Awake and alive

Humbly, I come to you

Seeking peace and freedom

And you give in abundant waters

Surrounding me

Attentive

10/12/16

Today I start over

I pull my dusty boots out from under my bed

I tie up my hair in a pleasant twist

My hands wrap tightly around my leather holster,
buckled securely at my midriff

I spend important minutes at the attentive heat of the
stovetop

I have the armor and sustenance I need to face these 24
hours I woke up to

Although I am an adult

I am cared for as a beloved child

Never never never never never alone

Nourished

10/24/16

The blankness of this sinkhole

Combines with these shards of coke bottles lining the sidewalks down down into

Parking garages at 2 a.m. after a late flight

Twisting my neck this way and that

And being pulled downward

Deep in the pain–shaped pool

My hair catches in the drain and I'm jerking through the filters

To the middle of court surrounded by strangers watching me cry

Turning my stomach

Being kicked on the floor of my heart

In the kitchen where I was raised with a well–aproned grandmother after my father was burned and crushed

Like my battered heart

Buoyant, I surface in the lake by the resort

In the still, cool air

Wrapped a warmed towel around my suit

Twist the trickling damp from my tresses

Set me in your safe cabin by the roaring hearth

In new linens sewn just for me

Nourish me with spiced apples and honey cakes, meats
from Morocco, and breads from your hands

I slowly become human again

And after a string of days like this

I became human again

Infertility

Wait, Go, Speak, Think, Shut Up, Breathe

6/3/17

Wait, go, speak, think, shut up, breathe

Borrowed trust from another age

Flavors of worship ring and rain

Heaven so appetizing and distant and close as sorrow

Mystery is how I walk

With bent branches and wicked words

Heart–blackening ripples of death and love pumping

Secrets, liars and lies, fables, and truth reminiscent of
latter worlds and former company

Echoed archangels about the room

Flowers are children breathing life and oxygen,
bringing hope and fear to each moment

Why can't I be free

Aches and belly aches and fragmented figments and
filaments and I behold light behind the glassware

Can't touch
Too much heat

Spelunking

7/29/17

Unglued in this moment

Second guessing

Fluctuating in & out

This back & forth tumble

Barreling down

Flipping, falling

Grabbing for the wall

Catching for a moment

Words etched in the pavement

FREEDOM and CONTENTMENT

Stop grasping for your saving

Reality is He has you

But you're repelling

Swirling mindfield veiling

You are held & holding

Weakened by the abrasions

Of swinging towards the sides of caves and

Breaking off a piece of faith I'm

Ready for this weak end

Welcomed to lean back on this string

Safe from weathering breeze

Trust is a highering thing

Waiting for measures of spring

Ribs

11/1/17

This was the first Halloween where I didn't want to see the children in their costumes. My heart was heavy. I didn't want to see the joy in the tiny faces I was unable to produce myself. I didn't want to see the cuteness, the innocence. It was too far from how I feel. This year has been a mixture of semi acceptance of the "i" word. This year was the first time I called it infertility. But my acceptance was only semi because I still believe in a God who can do anything He wants, and overarching I am so happy with the life He has blessed me with: with spouse and family. Yet, there is a pain that comes when something that is innate for most people is broken and unfixable for me. I have a tender heart towards tiny humans. My favorite job was a teacher's aide for 4-year-olds. I adore my nieces and nephews. But I just could not this year. This year, I wrapped a blanket around my body, and cocooned my heart.

I listened to a song whose lyrics rang, "I was young and running wide open," and I thought yes that's what it's like. When you are born into a safe family, your ribs are peeled back and you bare your heart to the world. As life kicks you, one-by-one you learn to bring those ribs back over in protection. When I was in my twenties, I went through counseling and safe experiences that helped me reopen my heart to the world. Since then, every disappointment with people has curled those bones back inward once more. I can't decide if my cynicism is wise or a hindrance or both. When enough beggars are frauds, you tend to stop feeding them. "I was young and running wide open." I think one day I will find out how to get back to a version of this.

Woman

Written in the waiting room
prior to being surprised to find out
I was pregnant for the first time.

5/16/18

A woman's body is like a tree

Bountiful, shady branches of shimmering green

Like arms stretching over the ones she loves

A woman's body is a twisted trunk

Memories of storms weathered etched into gnarled bark

Scars of good and bad entwined

A woman's body is like annual rings of life growing through all seasons, all weather

Like a historical document of truth, no lies are captured

A woman's body is an intricate root system—knows where the water is, where her family is; mapping deep and wide

Her reach is beyond what anyone can see

A woman's body is like a broken branch, severed from

ax, saw, or lightning

Imperfections leading to new blossoming fruit in uncovered places

And that fruit may drop

And that seed may wilt into the fragrant soil

And one day

A woman's body is like a tree

when water turns to vapor

Loss

Secret Places

6/30/18

Normally, she would escape to the cave, the hidden door carved from a tree stump hidden in the nest of the woods. Under the earth and behind nature's flesh she felt completely safe. Locked away in the precious secret place unsullied by human disturbance.

And He was there, always with eyes full of love and always behind the island stove in the tiny kitchen, frying fragrant dishes, sometimes sauces of caramelized onions, fresh herbs, creams, and fermented juices. She would flop down before him, sinking into the folds of the pillowy but rough, green couch cushions. Her tense demeanor always relieved by his eyes and his calm cooking. His normalcy during her storms was always anchoring to her soul.

But it all played out differently today.

Today when she stormed in, she didn't flop into the 70s avocado–colored davenport. She furiously cleared the island of spices, dishes, pots and pans, chopping boards and vegetables, cheese wheels, olives, figs and cured meats. Fire in her eyes danced on wet tears as she swiped feverishly with all of the strength in her shoulders, pushing the hand-spun ceramic mugs to the brick floor, shards splintering as handles broke free and corners rippled apart with the laws of physics. Wildly, her fists slammed as hard as they could on the wall shelves, destroying every stein glass, every tea cup, every vase and stoneware plate displayed. She ripped pillow fabric, shredding stuffing ‘till it floated in the air like fiber snow. She took a cleaver to the wall, sinking it deep into the drywall over and over, the last time so deep that her hand was briefly caught in the wall.

By the time she exhausted all her efforts, the only thing left intact in the very place she had found the most comfort was a twig-and-twine cross hanging from a thin nail behind the door, swinging gently with rhythmic creaking as it slowed to stopping.

And He had watched her calmly through this, knowingly, with hot tears, with a broken heart, with needles in his sides wishing there was something he could do to take her pain. He related to the begging to God for a different story. The destruction of personal self as your choices are held out of reach. The emptying of sobs until nothing is left to come out. The physical anguish of a grieving soul.

She couldn't look at him. Not yet. She couldn't slump into her corner of the sofa. She couldn't love or make peace or consider other angles or hope or think of the future or trust in the past or believe or embrace. She couldn't hear, couldn't swallow, couldn't slow her heartbeat, or relax the clenching of her stomach. Her sorrow enveloped her like the ivy that crawls upon undisturbed chimneys.

A Little Ripping

7/3/18

Everything's changed and nothing has changed

I knew you for less than 6 weeks

I had cautioned myself to play it safe and daily, but
soon was thinking of the future, a planner I am

Now instead of diapers in January, I'm changing my
bloody pads in June

Instead of feeding a tiny mouth, I'm delving into foods
I was avoiding for weeks

Instead of waking every two hours to nurse, I wake
every hour to the effects of the pill that clears the tissue

Morning dawns to the same beautiful life I had before
you

And nothing has changed, but everything has changed

You were potential, out of my control

Now you are slipping away in pieces, as if another
month of menses is clocking in per usual

I know I asked for part of this, but I didn't ask for this
part

I prepared myself and cautioned the few I told this to

Now, hardly anyone knows the slipping

We tie our hands together and grab each other's faces,
we drop the hot salt drops all over each other's
shoulders

We check in each moment

Even have calm normal conversation and laughter

Until another little damn breaks

A little cracking of the dike

A tiny tearing of the future

A little ripping of the hope

Untethered

7/20/18

Feeling untethered

Feeling unanchored

Feeling the roof roll away and the wind drag me upwards

I am uncertain of what will come next

Today was one where every other word was dark under my breath

Until he caught and held my gaze with love

I need to live in the second

Instead of prepping my mind for the conversations and questions

Or the self–razing reminders that to break the stigma you have to talk

I suppose a part of me needs to be real

While the other wants to be happy

But I am not fully happy

Don't even know how to rest

With the:

Be productive

Be real

Don't be bored

Accept that you have a short attention span for it's society that carved it

Learn to rest

Don't think about how satisfying it is to get lost in the work, in the solving a problem like only you can

It's full day one, it'll come

They just want to talk

And play

And look

And watch

And marvel

And cook

And you look across the table at each other wondering if the other is okay, will be okay

What is happening with my body

Is it broken for a reason

I like the days when I am not thinking of my body

And my focus is forward

And I feel good about myself and life

So many blessings around me yet

I see how someone can get trapped in the mind of it's not enough

Until they finally exhaust all their grasping

And realize the Only One that is enough

Swore He didn't leave

Didn't forsake

And when you said it is finished

Despite the release

You knew the sorrow that was still to come

But he's here, he's always here. Only he is always here

In the right place

In the exact place

In the right way

In the only way

Holding all of the truth and life

Streaming living water from his side

The Atmosphere Inside My Head

7/31/18

There is atmosphere inside my head

I can't seem to escape

Even if I could, there's the earth's atmosphere to break

Before I can see from that right perspective

There is a pressure system stirring in my head

My emotions at sea level are in flux

Will it be a dry or rainy day?

Will the humidity leak through my tear ducts?

Even if it did, I still have the earth's atmosphere

between me and from where I used to see

Twisted

8/29/18

Aching aching aching aching

I never will get to hold you because you never were

But you were

You changed my body

You changed my mind

You changed my relationships

You changed my future

You changed my hope

You changed my truth

Am I better than I was?

Briefly I was wholer

Now I am a twisted soft serve

Leaning, dripping

Aching, aching, aching

Can't

9/7/18

Cannot

No

Cannot cannot

Cannot

Go

Will not will not

Be able to

Hold

Composure composure

Feeling

Weak

Arms are feeling

Half

Asleep

Emotions hanging

Barely

On

Cannot smile

My power's

Gone

Cannot will not

Cannot

Go

Fountain

9/17/18

You are good to me

A kiss under the grapefruit tree

A pleasure of mental aperture

Wandering through the dark streets

Starry night

Caustic

10/22/18

Pent up not helping

Avoiding not working

Ignoring not possible

Opinions unwarranted, caustic

Truth is unclarified

Common ground seemingly impossible

7 billion perspectives and no one is thinking of mine

Please don't do this

Even if I agree with some of it

I can't see it that way

Please don't talk to me

About my rights

You don't know what I need

Never been in my shoes

No one is thinking of me

Abandoned Road

12/23/2018

I found myself on abandoned road

No light, no sound, no soul

A fearsome crawling down my neck

And a pound of flesh for toll

I whispered comforts to myself

“It’s not like this for good”

“I can make it through this horror:

friends, Deity say I could.”

The end of road I could not spy

A clammy mist obscured

But I kept walking down that road

Fighting thoughts unsure

I sensed a softness at my feet

warm peace enveloped me

I was still amid the dark

But had the sense to see

No sound but still I heard a voice

It clasped my hand in love

It cried my tears along with me

And never left my side

When through the terrible cold night

A tiny golden ray

A sliver of hope, barely there

But strong to light my way

I can't explain how one can feel alone but surrounded here

Embraced and safe, though danger's cuts leave one scarred and scared

I cannot understand how lost and ruined a wanderer can be

Yet saved and whole and lifted up into eternity

These truly aren't abandoned roads

That light dispelled the lies

For when the fog is lifted, see

My reflection in your eyes

My Shell

1/3/2019

Retreating into my shell

Where it is quiet and damp and warm

Like a still cavern, only natural echoes of cave-carving
water droplets mimic my breathing patterns

Safe solace

Surrounded by towering steeples of silica, icicles of
stone

My breath gets lost in the placid homeyness, fears
skitter away

Nothingness

Blankness

Air, warmth, and stable walls

I stroke the smooth and rough patches of limestone

As I sleep

Soft Pinks and Powder Blue

1/5/2019

Broken dreams

Borrowed themes

Chinking tea cups with destiny

Swaddled in empathy

Soft pinks

Harbor death's winks

Reaching for a cowards way through

A turbulent ocean of powder blue

Recalling days before

Being crushed by the closing door

Chasing gleaming thoughts of tethered three

One less is now negative me

I think I can get away

From thoughts that are stitched in to stay

Palo Verde

2/19/19

Palo Verde verde verde

Green green green

Smooth arms reaching gently to caress the

Tiny yellow confetti flowers

Crunching as I shuffle beneath the poles of green in the garden

How many Arizona memories are tied to the crispy floral raindrops tumbling down the avenue in the warm breeze?

Elixirs

3/20/19

Blank faces and elixirs

Shallow conversations and numbing humor

Sugar, sugar, carbs and sugar

Until the true craving palette is unearthed

Sorrow

Pure pounding-me-into-the-ground sorrow upon sorrow

Sorry for the reclipse

Sorry for the words you don't have the strength to say again

The sick time you don't have to take

The energy you don't have to expend on really embracing grief

12 months of sore heart is less than some, more than many

Why this story is not done is unclear

Washing

3/26/19

Thankfulness a wellspring

Gratefulness an ocean

A wonderful wave of washing, cleansing love crashing, breaking over me

The God who felt so distant

Is near

He takes my hand and walks with me

After I had been rushing—

A stroll

After I had been hungry—

A quiet dinner

Listening ears, loving eyes

And all the time, time, time.

The Traveler

6/2/2019

I used to travel far and wide, seemingly months between tears

Now I feel tethered to my sorrow

Never feel out of its zip code

Thinking I'm miles away then a trigger push and I am adjacent to yesterday's sadness, tomorrow's fear

Lord, bring back the joyous days

Stringed together unendingly

The grateful days

Thankful days

Right now the joy is bittersweet

Linked in molten metal like the heads and tails of a coin

But I'm still traveling under the shadow of your cloud by day and pillar of fire by night

Angels surrounding me

Nursing my wounds

Spiritual

Emotional

Thank you for your presence in the journey

Encourage

9/20/2019

Let the troubles and losses of your past

not be the weight on your shoulders

but be the stones lifting you higher.

Saved

2/5/2020

Your basic curmudgeon

Locked in a dungeon

Putrid and pungent

You made me regent

Thought I was all done

Though bought with Your own Son

Absorbing Your fragrance

You simmer and savor

Fire and water

Boiling together

Vapor the other

One with the Father

Spirit like Mother

Comfort and cover

Hid in Your shelter

Knitted together

My bones are willing

My spirit is failing

Sirens resounding

Asking for healing

You never leave me

Your power surrounding

Your goodness inside me

Break every binding

Tenderest mercies

Come up to meet me

Faith like the children

Clouds they are parting

Recalling the cycle

Of sorrow and favor

The prideful You humble

To bring us in closer

Oh, heavens declare it

Where ears can hear it

The Lord is my Temple

The broken run to It

She Silently Sits and Thinks

3/5/20

How her cycle tells tales

How she declines to verify the lies

Ever since the second death

She capped the tests and determined she would see one of two outcomes no matter her actions

She remembers how vigorously she guarded her temple, and how the enemy had already breached the barrier

The pendulum swings and she is nothing now. Not moving a finger to try, to see.

The future is out of her control. No use denying it.

when water turns to vapor

Pregnancy & Birth

when water turns to vapor

The Sun

7/24/20

Don't look into the sun

It will blind you

It will scar you

You can't distinguish its mass

Don't put your trust into the sun

You can't know it

Or understand it

Only watch the effects of it

On your body

On your mind

Don't long for the sun

It will burn you

It will hurt you

Just be satisfied standing nearby

For however long

Don't whisper to the sun

It can't tell you

It can see you

It can't give you what you need

Don't imagine the sun

Thoughts are not truth

Feelings are not facts

Dreams are not destiny

Don't ignore the sun

The sun matters

The sun interacts

The sun changes

Don't fear the sun

The sun doesn't fear you

The sun is trusting, longing, whispering, imagining,

listening...

In Process

10/26/2020

The gift of time passing

Painted black nails

grow out, then disappear into a sliver at the edge of fingertips

A discarded apple

decays into the rocks until it is indistinguishable

The clear mark in time then

changes out of your control

Something comforting about processes ongoing

Flowers and vines on a coffee shop wall in various states of being: buds, blooms, and dry, crispy, brown death

At any given time, our existence vibrates in alternate states

The Table Before Me

10/27/2020

Fear

Reminders of the past

distract from present joy

A well treaded dirt path to a lovely open valley

distant blue peaked mountains

In the middle of

web–covered burrows, tarantula nests

Pregnancy after loss

Stand in awe at the table before, although not blind to the presence of enemies

What It's Like

2/15/2021

I drive, breakfast

The rearview mirror, the carseat

My abdomen moves, my son

Ripped and taped by previous loss, victory unfolding with heavenly hope

Today is all we have, permission and grace in sorrowful and fearful moments

We hold each other's hands, we touch my stomach.

We tell my belly, "We want you to know that we love you," no matter what the day brings,

because we have witnessed what the day brings

Holding on to hope is not without rope burns and blisters and blood

Motherhood

Not Big Enough

6/2/2021

The starlight and moon glow fell through the dark,
It landed with thrusters right on my heart.

It opened a gateway to a world never seen;
The starlight was you and the darkness was me.

You emerged from the quiet and made the blank full,
cut through the shadows on the globe of my soul.

You pitched your flag and claimed me as yours,
brighter and stronger than gravity's force.

No billions of lightyears could ever contain
the swell of my heart when I see your face.

I had a dream and oh how it came true;

My dream was a baby, that baby is you.

Little Moments

9/24/2021

Little moments

I see it in your eyes

The poetry of these little moments

Your curiosity

Your play

I want to meet you here in these little moments

I explode like a shooting star

When your laughter cracks the air

Each a precious gift

these little moments

One day I will look behind me

Not at any of my so-called accomplishments

No

I will be filled to overflowing

Remembering these little moments

Comfort

9/26/2021

Silence

Rain

The gentle rise and fall of baby's chest

Perfect

Temperature cool, body warm

Comfort in each other's presence

Strivings Cease

10/10/2021

Sit with this

I'm sitting with this

This enlightenment

So light, so heavy

It weighs my heart down like an anchor

To the bottom of the sea

If forgiveness was an ocean

Then purpose is the worship of the one who commands the waves

Sitting with the thought of your broken pieces

Not focused on mine for my son

But on yours for your daughter

Your honored one

Feeding the thousands with pieces of you

Come to dwell with humans forever

Your Spirit in me cries, "Abba, Father"

I am to come to You like my son calls to me

Just be with me

I can't do this work thing on my own

Strivings cease and good news is not an opinion piece

It's witnessing the alive King now

We are a blip on His timeline of always

Not an accident

Purposeful love

To receive and to share

Strivings cease

Versions of Me

11/7/2021

I'm all those people

All those versions of me you have witnessed through the years

Iterations through seasons, sorrows, celebrations, sunsets, and sonnet

The account of me you believe depends on what you've experienced and what we've shared

There they all are acting in unison

A water ballet, one featured, many submerged kicking at the sky, bubbles exhaling, sharing the air

Thank you for knowing me

Thank you for keeping me

A Whisper

11/26/2021

A whisper to me

A silent prayer

Trust and peace

Know You're there

When things don't look like

I feel they should

You're still with me

'Cause You said You would

Ghosts

1/9/22

Ghosts of my past flit around in night vision

Grayscale foreground white sheets and moth wings

Flickers of blurry movement and smeared motion but for a second and vanish

Superstitious thoughts

My Birthday

1/21/22

This birthday is different than all before

Because I see your face, Mom

I see your pain, Mom

I see your wisdom, Mom

All these years gone by

And I understand a glimpse

I understand your first year with me

My birth day was not just the beginning of my story

It was the middle of yours

And so much more

Today represents years of balancing lessons with independence

Shouldering loads

Being the "adult" when no one feels like it

Making decisions and weighing options without
information just with instinct and love

And oh the fear

and guilt

and heightened joy

It may be my birth day,

but happy birth day to you, Mom

Emotional

1/27/22

These power struggles between holding on and letting go

Of moving forward and standing still

Of grasping and releasing

Your newfound independence brings independence to me, too

And I will cherish our precious bonding time

It's all so hard and easy

It's learning and loving you

It's a ripping away of selfishness and a striving for self-care

We're finding our way

Together and solo

Your first steps will also be mine

I've never done this before

But watching you

think,
listen,
obey,
explore,
talk,
sing,
whine,
howl,
grab,
throw,
pinch,
climb,
stand,
point,
sign

every little movement is being established

You're excited and needing reassurance

I am proud and emotional

when water turns to vapor

Afterword

A Pregnancy Loss Story

1/18/2019

Warning: Some descriptions may be disturbing to some readers.

The First Journey

It was a Wednesday in May when I went to my annual well-woman's exam. I had been putting it off because we had a lot going on, and I was constantly tired from my 10-hours-a-day summer work schedule. I had a few questions I wanted to ask, but otherwise was simply looking forward to crossing it off of my list. I don't know why, but I apologized for coming in when I was still spotting from my period (like she hasn't seen it all before), but I did. In your late thirties you start to care less about what other people might think. Because my cycle was irregular, I couldn't ever predict when I would be clear, so I didn't reschedule my annual exam like I may have in the past.

In the cold room, I sat on the table, covered only by a pink paper vest and white paper tissue sheet, leaning in as I talked with my Nurse Practitioner. I had been seeing this NP for many years, because she was always open to questions despite the signs above her head that said to "schedule a second appointment if you have concerns outside your annual exam." Something about billing the visit correctly, they stated.

It's a funny thing—human hope. How it can spiral down a well, be seemingly lost forever, and then can surprise you by peeking its head out unexpectedly.

I had been trying to accept that my body was atypical. My menstrual cycle was rarely regular. I had been loosely diagnosed with PCOS (Polycystic Ovarian Syndrome) four years prior and recently saw cystic activity on my ovaries. I was approaching 40 and, although my husband of 12 years and I were not trying, I never was pregnant despite not preventing it for a number of years. In that visit, I relayed to my NP that I knew I couldn't control everything, but not being in control when it pertains to my body was making me feel down. Thinking out loud, she talked through the possibilities, asking if I was interested in taking natural hormones that could at least possibly regulate my cycle. I said yes, as trying something different felt like moving forward.

It's a funny thing—human hope. How it can spiral down a well, be seemingly lost forever, and then can surprise you by peeking its head out unexpectedly.

In one of those "cover your ass" moves, my NP said she needed a urine sample to test for pregnancy before prescribing me hormones. It felt hurtful. Like, why rub in my face the exact reason you're prescribing them in the first place? She left the room so I could don my clothes before I exited the exam room and crossed the hall to the restroom.

I had already emptied my bladder prior to my exam, so it was a struggle to provide a sample. After some time, I returned to the room with a meager offering, and sat down next to her while she used an eyedropper to activate the test.

I had personally taken a number of pregnancy tests over the years. Every test I peed on was negative. My body never really had distinct or obvious routines, even when I attempted to track it, so it never relayed any reliable or understandable data. I didn't know how to trust my body's signals.

Saying I was shocked doesn't do it justice.

"See, that's why we do these tests," she said slowly. I was confused. "Come again?" I needed more information to understand what was going on, and I saw it—plain as day—the test was positive. Saying I was shocked doesn't do it justice. I had been feeling physically off, and had taken a home test about two weeks prior and it was negative. I wasn't throwing up. I was still spotting from what I thought was my last period. My NP reveled in the irony of my rollercoaster of a visit as she sent a message to my pharmacist cancelling a prescription I was on. I remember she briefly touched on the fact that miscarriage was still a risk and 12 weeks is usually where people breathe a sigh of relief. She handed me my positive pregnancy test in plastic bag, and congratulated me.

I was so staggered, that I didn't hear her ask me to stop at the lab on the way out to get blood work. When I got to my car, I called my husband to get his dinner order, but waited to tell him in person because most pressingly I NEEDED TO EAT SOMETHING. I picked up dinner, mind spinning, repeatedly looking in my purse at the positive test in the hazmat bag. Once home, my husband asked how it went and I told him I'd tell him in a minute. We sat down, prayed, got a few bites in then I calmly told him exactly as it happened, as if there was no surprising punch line at the end. When I got to the part where she said, "See, that's why we do these tests," I pulled out the pee stick and showed him. We hugged. We were astounded and later decided we were cautiously optimistic—even happy.

I went back to the physician's office that Friday to provide the blood work I missed. My NP called me from home Friday evening before the weekend to make sure I knew my HCG levels put my pregnancy at 5 weeks, and that "spotting is not abnormal. I wanted to call you because I know how your mind works and you would worry." She wasn't incorrect, but thankfully

Monday's blood work showed the HCG level continuing to rise—a great sign.

My husband and I decided to keep the remarkable news to ourselves for the time being, seeing as my body had never been predictable in feminine ways. But soon silence became a burden, and felt like we were lying to everyone who asked us, "What's new?" Yes, we enjoyed our secret, but keeping my mouth closed about the huge change in our lives felt like all I was really doing about it was mentally mitigating bad things that might happen, and not enjoying my pregnancy. I had already stopped eating my favorite food (sandwiches with deli meat) and packed my lunch bag with tasteless organic boiled eggs, plain raw carrots, and fruit. I avoided standing in front of microwaves, breathing wood stain fumes, exhaust, and cigarette smoke. I was thinking through our upcoming trip to Montana, how I would choose the TSA pat down instead of the scanner, have to stand up and stretch legs on the airplane to avoid blood clots, might have to stop to pee on the drive from the airport to the cabin, avoid the shooting range for lead particulates and high decibels, and buy maternity clothes. Everything had changed and most of it seemed focused on avoiding problems. And when avoiding problems, one is fixated on problems.

All in all, it wasn't possible to keep it to ourselves for the full first trimester. Out of necessity, the first person we told was the chiropractor the Monday after we found out, because I had a bimonthly adjustment and I wanted the doctor to be aware. He offered congratulations, but I cautioned him due to it being so early on. I don't know if he thought it would be reassuring – it wasn't – but he told us his wife had a miscarriage and later got pregnant and sometimes the body needs a practice round.

The second person I told out of obligation was my boss, but for an unfortunate reason. I was bleeding red (not just spotting) and I had to make a last minute ultrasound appointment mid-workday, causing me to leave the office spontaneously. Despite my facial cues, she was overjoyed, but I warned her that we're not ready to celebrate.

This was the pattern each time I revealed the miracle, and not at all how I wanted it to go—sharing this news that I was pregnant for the first time.

Becoming Real

The day of the red bleeding, my husband met me for the spur-of-the-moment ultrasound. The sonogram showed an early heart flutter. We were reassured that the bleeding—though disconcerting—was normal. They said it was measuring 5 weeks, 5 days, and the estimated due date was 3 days before my next birthday.

Standing outside the OB office in the warmth of the Arizona sun, I asked my husband tearfully if he minded if I told one person—whether my Mom, a sister, or my best friend—someone who has experienced pregnancy and of whom I could ask questions. It had been a nerve-wracking day. He agreed. I decided I would share the news with my closest girlfriend, a mother of three.

She was happy for me, but able to be emotionally level to how I felt—exactly the emotional support I needed.

The next time I saw her, we were taking her kids to a public pool. They were old enough to swim on their own, so we sat on the edge of the pool, and I told her the story. She was happy for me, but able to be emotionally level to how I felt—exactly the emotional support I needed, and not what I felt some of our family members would be able to do. She said she'd pray for me which I hadn't realized before was a major comfort that I was lacking. My husband and I didn't have anyone praying for us at that point, even though we used to have a tight-knit community of faith. Time had passed since we lived in a traditional Christian community.

That month, we had planned a trip to see my sisters who live in northern Arizona—one in Prescott, one in Flagstaff. I agonized over telling them, but my husband and I agreed to wait to tell the family. It was so hard to sit next to my oldest sister in a Mexican restaurant in Prescott, share chips and salsa with her husband and four kids, and not let her in on the biggest and latest news of my life. I justified it by thinking about how, for the time being, it was wise to limit the chances of someone spilling the beans on social media. When we got to Flagstaff, we spent time with my 2nd oldest sister, her husband and two kids. My sister herself experienced a miscarriage in the past, and I was compelled to ask what week of her pregnancy it had happened. She answered me, then asked if I was pregnant. I looked at my husband, and we conceded the truth. She was somewhat emotionally at my level, but on the other hand asked "happy sister" questions that confused my emotions. How can I talk about a positive future with a child, when I'm just trying to get through the next day to see this pregnancy progress correctly? She ended up sharing our news with her husband who reassured us with a doctor quote from his experience with their formerly medically compromised, now healthy 5-year-old first born, "heartbeat is everything." I felt relieved. As we returned to the valley, I was able to cautiously be positive.

I found myself grinning a knowing look at my reflection in the mirror.

As the days rolled by, despite the exhaustion and shortness of breath I experienced, I found myself grinning a knowing look at my reflection in the mirror. I sneaked into the maternity section of a department store and debated over buying a work outfit for the future. We were still trying to play it day-by-day, but I gave in to the purchase because I knew I was leading a training at work in the next month, and expected to want to hide a growing waistline.

Then I started to get bolder. I thought it would be a good exercise in faith to plan a party to tell my siblings the news. If the pregnancy didn't last, at least we would be together, I thought. Against my better judgment, and because I just wanted to do something typically happy, I ordered custom t-shirts for my husband and I to wear at the party that said "Mom, est. 2019" and "Dad, est. 2019."

During this time, I felt hungry all day and night, and tried to constantly have something in my stomach to avoid any inkling of nausea. We got ants in our upstairs bathroom because I left saltines out for mid-night snacking. Organic fruit snacks and peppermint candies were always in my purse. My coworker must have noticed me eating all the time, and getting up to use the bathroom more often. Honestly, it was getting ridiculous. After work I would go home and share my thoughts and stories of my pregnancy symptoms and my husband and I would start to dream a little about adding to our little family of 2 our little secret 3rd.

My mom was overjoyed.

At our second ultrasound at 6 weeks 6 days (the first official OB appointment), the sonogram showed we now had a bean–shaped embryo and they confirmed there was still a heartbeat. That second appointment was a dose of positivity. I was torn inside between reining in my feelings through all 12 weeks of the first trimester, and sharing the news excitedly. Somehow that night, we talked ourselves into telling our parents. We web-conferenced my husband's folks and held up the ultrasound pic and got an amazing reaction of shouts and tears. We asked them to not share because we didn't want anything on social media. We drove to my parents and showed them the ultrasound. My mom was overjoyed, and though we signaled them that it was too early on, she was compelled to crochet a beautiful baby blanket. When she brought it over wrapped with baby wrapping paper, I was afraid someone would see it. It felt like the wrong time to receive gifts—as if it was tempting fate to pull the rug out from under me. It gave me mixed feelings, but I thanked her and admitted, "You're the grandma, you can do what you want."

We tried to take it one day at a time, but I also didn't want to miss documenting the details—in the event that it was a successful pregnancy. I tentatively purchased a pregnancy journal from Barnes and Noble—holding it face down as I stood in line for the register, as if I might run into someone I knew.

I also had a Mayo Clinic book about pregnancy, and I would read to my husband what was going on each week. Looking at the illustrations of the size and growth of the baby in the womb, week-by-week, you imagine you get a peek inside at what's going on. Yet, no one can truly tell you what is actually going on.

Foreshadowing

One of my colleagues at work told me a story about some trouble she was having with ducks making a mess of her pool deck. She respects nature and was working with the animal service to relocate the ducks safely, but the service had regulations they had to follow. One such rule was that they couldn't remove adult ducks. The intruding group of birds started as a mother with a nest of eggs. My colleague wouldn't handle them herself so as to not contaminate the eggs with her smell and cause the mother to abandon their care. Soon all the eggs but one hatched, and the mom began to treat the pool as her own private lake. She would swim with the ducklings trailing blissfully behind, and they all made a terrible mess of her deck with their waste. The animal service said they were now able to intervene, as the mallards were an endangered species, yet they would only remove the babies, not the mother. They assured my colleague that they already had surrogate mother ducks to care for the offspring, and removed the ducklings and left. They suggested she leave her gate open and maybe the mother duck would leave on her own. Unfortunately, that's not what happened.

She was left swimming blindingly in her loss.

From the time the animal service took the babies away, the mommy duck stared out at the pool the entire day without moving or quacking. Seemingly frozen. How heart-wrenching is that? She was looking for her babies that were no longer there. She didn't understand. My colleague gave the mother a day undisturbed to mourn her loss. The next day, the mother duck pushed the unborn egg into the pool and began swimming with it. It was like she couldn't accept that her babies were gone. She was left swimming blindingly in her loss. Eventually, the mom flew away.

The Second Journey

In my 10th week, I wasn't feeling hungry and on the edge of nausea any longer. A mixture of fear and relief accompanied the change. Instead of telling my Mom I was scared like I truly was, I tried to adjust my attitude and be positive. I texted her, "I'm hoping it's a good sign," knowing full well I wasn't yet at the end of the first trimester when you're supposed to feel better.

"I'm not in pain, but I think we should go to the Emergency Room."

Early on that Saturday morning before it was light out, my bladder woke me and I noticed moderate bleeding. I had been spotting for over 7 weeks, but this time I noticed a clear change. I calmly woke my husband, stating, "I'm not in pain, but I think we should go to the Emergency Room." I texted our moms, my sister and my friend and asked them to pray. We got dressed and drove in the dark to the hospital right down the street from our house. Most of the medical personnel were personable and helpful enough to mitigate my fears as time passed between tests and diagnosis. One male nurse took my blood, and placed a needle in my arm in the event I would later need drugs or an IV. Another male nurse took my urine to get tested. I was told to put on a gown with nothing from the waist down. The night shift doctor and a female nurse took me to another room for a physical exam. The exam showed my cervix was slightly open—which he said wasn't definitive, but was a bad indicator. The doctor took me back to the ER room where we began and a third male nurse pushed in a sonogram cart. The doctor put gel on my belly, and proceeded with the first external abdominal ultrasound I had in my pregnancy. He concluded that he couldn't find a heartbeat and needed to call in a vaginal ultrasound tech.

My husband and I were left alone for a while. At one point, another female nurse connected me to a blood pressure monitor cuff on my arm and a blood oxygen monitor on my finger. Every so often the monitor would beep like "something's wrong," but no one came in. I suppose my blood pressure was spiking because of stress. I was sitting helplessly on the hospital bed, bleeding some onto the gown and the bed pad and waiting for answers—the full truth. We had been told my cervix was slightly open and the external ultrasound machine couldn't find what the internal one had found twice a month ago. We were left to worry, wonder and to wait for the labs to be processed and the technician to come. I used the bathroom multiple times from nervousness, but to get to the bathroom down the hall, I had to unhook the monitor leads. In the hallway, I passed an inmate in an orange jumpsuit surrounded by Sheriff's deputies getting care for seizures. I was glad I apparently wasn't emergent myself. Even if the life inside me was, no one treated us like that. No one rushed around trying to resuscitate or save anything. In the restroom, it was frustratingly difficult to do my business. The empty needle in my arm had been placed where I couldn't bend my elbow without pain, and the wire from my finger monitor on my left hand hung down. I was slowly wearing down.

The ultrasound tech finally arrived and she was nice enough, but didn't offer me much information, only directed me to raise my hips off the table or be prepared for more pressure. Her silence otherwise spoke volumes. I turned my head away from her face and from my husband's concerned expression staring at the monitor that I couldn't see. I strained at the clock, choking back tears of knowing what I was going to hear from the doctor after he read the scans.

He claimed it would be over in two days, and directed me to proceed with life as normal.

The female technician left, and we waited longer. We were at the hospital 3–4 hours before a new day shift doctor and the second female nurse came in with all the results and his diagnosis. He told us it was an "inevitable miscarriage." We thought we were at 10-weeks but the measurements were consistent with 8-weeks. He claimed it would be over in two days, and directed me to proceed with life as normal, even suggesting I should be able to attend work on Monday. Upon further discussion he offered to provide me with a doctor's excuse through Tuesday in case "emotionally" I wasn't ready to go back to work. He directed me to follow up with my OB on Monday and prescribed Naproxen for the pain. They left the room and we grasped each other and cried. I remember saying I'm so sorry over and over again. My husband said not to say that, but it just came out.

Once the needle was removed, the monitors were detached, I was offered a new sanitary pad, and I got dressed and we walked to the car. In the light of morning, wearing my normal clothes, bleeding like a normal period and not in pain, it felt surreal. Isn't bad medical news always associated with pain? I was crying. I was in shock. And I realized I had to write the follow-up text to our mothers, my sister, and my friend. I felt like I had to word it in a way that was clinical and could "let them down" easily. I tried to read it aloud to my husband but broke down between every other word:

"Not what we wanted to hear. Nature found something wrong in the development of the fetus resulting in fetal demise (no heartbeat). I'm going through a miscarriage. Thank you for praying."

The Third Journey

I felt I should have known earlier, should have trusted the fear that I was told to ignore.

But here I was now, wondering how I could be hungry for breakfast and not be in pain when I was losing this pregnancy? It may have been denial at the time.

That weekend, we drowned our senses in a lot of television and ate our fill of comfort food. I went through many sanitary pads. I passed some large tissue or a clot, but really wasn't sure. No medical personnel showed me what to look for, so I had to web-search to get answers to my questions.

The weekend was waning, and as Monday approached I had to deal with the fact that I was to have a follow up appointment with an OB yet I didn't have an OB yet, not really anyway. Just three days prior I had been researching new practices, and had made an upcoming appointment with a very experienced Midwife I had never met. I had told my regular practice I was looking for someone else. I was worried I totally burned that bridge, but considering everything that happened, I decided I preferred going back to the OB I already met at the office that already had all my medical records.

I felt the worst emotional sorrow I had ever experienced.

At the appointment the OB consoled me in the unemotional way only a clinician can. She said it would be another week or so through this process and it would be like a heavy period. I asked if I would see anything and she said nothing that would look like a baby.

I cried harder than I have ever cried, felt the worst emotional sorrow I had ever experienced. I was losing the life inside me physically, as well as grieving a tremendous loss emotionally. And mentally, what do you do when there's no funeral, no gravesite? My boss was understanding of my situation, and I took sick time from work that full week. How do you explain this situation in the cold confines of a "human capital management" system? Instead of "sick time" I could instead select "bereavement leave," but then I would have to state their relation to me. There was no way in hell that I could select "child" from a damn drop-down menu. It had been a whirlwind 2 months finding out and accepting I was pregnant, gaining hope then losing it. At the time and despite the fact that it had once had a heartbeat, I was struggling to even see it as a child. My beliefs about it all were still evolving.

That weekend, the bleeding appeared to be subsiding, so I planned to go to work the very next Monday afternoon, barring any bad news from my OB appointment that a.m. At my morning appointment, the NP who knew me for a long time came into my ultrasound and both her and the office ultrasound tech who I had been getting to know, both expressed emotion. I had told my husband he didn't need to come at this point. It was no longer a pregnancy, and I was expecting an "all clear." I wanted to treat it like a regular OBGYN visit. Yet, as I watched on the monitor as the tech checked the progression of the miscarriage, I was distraught to see that after 9 days since the hospital, there was still a baby–shape in my uterus. The OB I knew was on vacation for the Fourth of July, so another of the practice's OBs gave me my options: (1) let nature continue in it's timing, (2) take medication to stimulate delivery of the tissue, or (3) schedule a surgery (Dilation & Curettage). At first I asked for the D&C, but she said it would be at a hospital and not in the office, so I opted for the medication instead, and at my request I was prescribed Misoprostol to finish passing the fetal tissue. In the car I called my husband, crying. I had wanted this all to be over and to go back to work, but it hadn't really even begun! I texted my boss to let her know I wasn't coming in that day. And, because there was some recent controversy in the news with this particular pharmaceutical and a Walgreens employee, I drove to CVS. I hoped I wouldn't experience any more conflict than what I was already going through.

The medication Misoprostol is 24-hours worth of pills to start labor. Within a few hours of the first dose it should begin labor and was expected to finish the hardest part within 48 hours. This had me expecting the process to be over by mid-week. Practically speaking, my sick time was dwindling, so I had added pressure to complete this soon. I gave permission for my mom and sister to tell my other 6 siblings so they could know what was going on and pray for us.

I experienced the worst physical pain of my life.

That night, my youngest sister and her husband brought my little nephew and niece over, but I had to excuse myself as the cramps started to get too strong to hide my discomfort from the kids. As they departed, I retreated upstairs and for the next hour I experienced the worst physical pain of my life. I was cramping so hard, I couldn't pee or defecate—though I felt I needed to do both—everything in my abdomen was in knots. Then all of the sudden, I had a little gush of watery liquid from my vagina, and felt overwhelming relief—a complete release of the muscle tension. That evening and through the night, and over the next day and a half, I passed a lot of blood, clots/tissue, something large that looked like a rotten tampon, and a flesh–colored oval with a black dot. The oval, skin-colored tissue looked like a fetus' head that I saw in a Google image search that I never dreamed I would ever be looking up. When you're going through something like this, you need all the information you can get, and unfortunately my OB provided not even a pamphlet. But I wanted to understand. I wanted to know what my body was doing, what was going on inside me. When I saw that tissue, I mustered my courage and reached in the dirty toilet water to get it out, but it was flat and hollow, and slipped out of my fingers. After those 48 hours of labor, I continued to stay home from work, catching up on work email a few hours each day, as I felt up to it. In the weeks that followed, I continued to need to take additional time away for follow-up doctor appointments.

The Fourth Journey

Everything after that 48-hours was the worst "firsts." First time back at the chiropractor after I alerted him to the sorrowful news via a preemptive email – the eye contact, the "I'm sorry." The first time receiving mail that was meant for an expectant mother and father – the Mom & Dad t-shirts I bought for the sibling reveal party. There was the first time back in the office, though my boss had completely understood and treated me professionally, keeping my privacy. The first time seeing all my siblings together, at the BBQ I had previously planned so we could reveal the joyous news. Instead, I got a sympathy card. The first time seeing my husband's family on our trip to Montana where we were going to tell his brother & his kids good news, but instead spent a tear–filled evening with his folks talking about the loss.

I must mention the good that's come, too.

But, I must mention the good that's come, too, as everyday is entwined with sweet & sour, roses and thistles: Talking with my sisters and girlfriends about each of their miscarriages has made me feel less alone in the female–side of the experience. Our parents were kind enough to give us space when we needed it. I got to see so much kindness from my brothers-in-law, nephew, and niece. Plus those who gave us permission to be whatever we truly are and truly feel in our grief, gave us such a gift of freedom with their words.

Frustrations still abound, though. A coworker saying, "It was for the best." Or the numerous, "Are you going to try again or be open to another pregnancy?" The feeling of screaming in your head, "F**k!" to everything and everybody all day long. The being afraid of becoming someone who thinks of suicide as a valid option. Like the mama duck slipping the stillborn egg in the pool and swimming around with it, one can drown in their heartbreak. You can feel so personally alone. Like a ghost—the feeling of unburied, unfinished. How does one grieve?

But the greatest blessing through this process is seeing even more strongly how I have the most amazing husband who has cried with me and carried me. We both recognize that only I held this in my body.

Only I was in the bathroom watching as that potential life leaked out of my womb. Only I reached into the waste to see if I could glimpse the form of a baby. But he was there with his strong arms and wise words of love. He experienced the loss in his way. I pray I can give him the support he needs, too.

Looking Back

When it's all over, what do you do with the sonogram pictures, the barely begun baby book, that bottle of prenatal vitamins, the new mom bag of samples from the OB's office, the baby blanket and the personalized shirts? What do I do when my friend has her baby? Or when milestones in time pass? What will happen on January 18, formerly our due date? My husband and I talk of getting a shared tattoo to remember, but what should that look like, and should we constantly be thinking about it? What do I make of the distance felt between words I thought God said and then the moment they seemingly turn dry and crumble into the wind? I am glad that faith is boomeranging back to be a comfort. For a time there, I could not look at Him. I still don't understand, but I do still believe Jesus never left me.

Now that I'm not bleeding, although I'm glad, it's sad, too. It is finished, yet my weight bears the memories by way of a couple extra pounds around the middle. A month after the ER, I still continue to go in for blood draws to ensure my HCG levels keep declining down to nothing. It's over yet the ripples still reverberate in my body. I don't expect to ever fully be the same again.

I shouldn't have had to do my own research, because nothing was given to me – not from the ER and not from the OB's office.

Now that the event has passed, I can reflect on what support was missing. I wish I had been provided a chart of what I might expect with the miscarriage: What was happening, what the stages are, and what I will see slipping out my body. I shouldn't have had to do my own research, because nothing was given to me – not from the ER and not from the OB's office. Before, during, and after my miscarriage, I had researched and heard information from health professionals that I wasn't aware of: 25% of known early pregnancies are lost. I was informed that some people wait until 14-weeks to tell people they are pregnant and 20-weeks to tell their work. I learned that there is always a chance of loss and nothing is 100%. Other facts I learned include at 10-weeks the embryo is considered a fetus when all the organs form. Other names for miscarriage include spontaneous abortion. There are multiple types of miscarriage including: threatened, inevitable, incomplete, complete, and missed. And, if you lose the baby after 20-weeks, it's called stillbirth.

Three Months Later

I finished the above account of my miscarriage in August of 2018. It's November now, and I can't believe where my heart is at. The days where I break down are less frequent, though I feel I think about my experience almost as often as I first did. There is a new feeling I have that is unexplainable: Gratefulness.

I am thankful that I held a potential life in my body. That it was mine. That no one can take that from me. It will always be a part of me. I am even thankful for the new shape of my waist, because it reminds me I was pregnant, that it really happened, even if it was just 10 weeks.

My husband said the most reassuring thing to me, "I am with you."

In early September, I was unable to attend a close friend's baby shower. Through a waterfall of tears, I explained to my husband how I felt I "should" be a certain way, but "couldn't." It wasn't in my capacity, and I would only distract from their happy day to hear what was going on in my life. My husband said the most reassuring thing to me, "I am with you." Isn't that all we really can receive during those times? The sense that you don't have to change, but you are not alone.

I know what is coming. January 18th was to be my due date. I expect to take a personal day. I expect to be a complete mess. I expect to be inconsolable (why should I be consoled?). My husband and I looked at the ultrasound pictures last night. The tiny shape. The heartbeat waveform. Our little Bean. I refer to it as a baby sometimes now. It's shorthand in our society. Pregnant = baby. I have more hopeful days now. Maybe a complete pregnancy, and whole baby will happen to us in the future (if God wills). I am no longer angry with God. I was humbled to be reminded that I can never put God in a box nor should I ever compare God to what I've experienced from humans. I believe I was given the latitude to get here by those who gave me permission to feel however I felt and be angry.

Closing Thoughts

If you're reading this and you're going through this, or just went through this, or have been through this multiple times, I ache for you. I wish for you to know that you won't always be walking through the graveyard of emotions. There is more to this complex life, and there will be new days, new experiences, and there is reason to believe in hope.

If you are interested in getting support or supporting this cause, please visit: *pregnancylossdirectory.com or rtzhope.org.*

Afterword

when water turns to vapor

Acknowledgements

It is important for me to acknowledge some people who have played no small role in helping me personally, academically, and otherwise reach the finish line on this publication. Please forgive any unintentional omissions.

My mom, author MaryBeth Roosa who has always been my writing and spiritual inspiration—I want to be like you. My brother-in-law, James Koenig of Freelance Fridge, who was a wellspring of advice, and provided formatting assistance for both the interior and exterior. My sister-in-law Desirae Roosa who found time between working a full-time job, parenting two exceptional children, and working on her own manuscript to review mine. Bryce Bickham, Jamie Drayton, Sarah Garone, MaryBeth Roosa, and Bekah Thompson for providing feedback and support.

The endorsers who provided advance praise—Valerie R. Meek, Lynne Renee Maxcy, Pastor Jodi Rodgers, Marcus Chinn—your selfless contributions humble me.

English and Creative Writing professors Joshua Rathkamp and Jeremy Venema who put the tools in my hands to better express the vastness of emotions that is the human experience. Donna Eames, my favorite junior high English teacher who simultaneously kindled my passion for writing by allowing me to work on a school newsletter *and* got me out of physical education class—both for which I am incredibly grateful.

The subscribers and readers of punandquill.wordpress.com who made me feel like my words could make a difference for someone.

The individuals who openly shared with me their stories of loss which in turn allowed me to find my courage to share mine. The friends and family members who walked with me in my darkest times and celebrated with me in the most joyous moments. My Pregnancy After Loss Support (PALS) group that provided both a shoulder to lean on and a flashlight when things were especially cloudy. The Return to Zero: Hope organization for not only offering validation and resources, but for taking action in a space where it is needed most. D. Kiley Krekorian Hanish, Founder of Return to Zero: HOPE, who connected me with Elizabeth O'Donnell, Founder & CEO of Aaliyah in Action—an amazing organization that provides care boxes to comfort families who have experienced perinatal loss, neonatal loss, or infant death.

Sarah Zimmerman, who didn't know it, but provided a healing space for me like only she can through a collaborative outlet with comedy writing. Liz Feldman, Christina Applegate, and Linda Cardellini for crafting a story called Dead to Me that offered a strangely comforting portrayal of anger and grief at the same time I was walking that road.

Binders, for advice and support. Tucker Max and Scribe Media for sharing step-by-step how to self publish. Shane Siebold, for his Public Relations expertise.

To Jesus, for letting me be mad at God, never leaving me, and giving me such a gift in my husband and son.

To my husband, Bryce, who—when I didn't think I could make it through—would be standing there, outside the shower where I was crying my eyes out, with a warm towel from the dryer to wrap around my body. There is no one like you, baby.

Finally, to my dear Benjamin Bickham who I have the indescribable pleasure of calling son, and the great honor of hearing call me mama.

Author Biography

Joy R. Bickham is the author of the blog Pun and Quill which has 3,525 all–time views and 213 followers reaching 1,456 readers in 36 nations. She is also co-creator of How Not To Podcast, available on YouTube.

Joy received awards in local and regional academic creative writing competitions: 3rd Place in Poetry for "Taste, Breathe, See," and Honorable Mention in Poetry for "Hid in a Soft–Sided Suitcase." She has penned multiple unproduced comedic works, including: "Emmie and the Alien," an original feature and "Childish," an original single-camera, half-hour television pilot.

She grew up and resides in Mesa, Arizona with her husband of 16 years, 1-year-old son, and extended family.

In her spare time, she enjoys cool weather, warm carbohydrates, and chuckling at Mischief Comedy.

Made in the USA
Middletown, DE
17 November 2022

15050942R00089